Essay to Write?

Second Edition

BRENDAN HENNESSY

howto books

First published as *Writing Successful Essays*

1857038355

How to Books Ltd,
3 Newtec Place, Magdalen Road,
Oxford OX4 1RE, United Kingdom
Tel: 01865 793806   Fax: 01865 248780
email: info@howtobooks.co.uk
www.howtobooks.co.uk

First edition, 2000
Second, revised and expanded edition, 2002

British Library Cataloguing in Publication Data.
A catalogue record for this book is available from
the British Library.

Edited by Diana Brueton
Cover design by Baseline Arts Ltd., Oxford
Produced for How To Books by Deer Park Productions
Typeset by Anneset, Weston-super-Mare, Somerset
Printed and bound by Bell & Bain, Glasgow

NOTE: The material contained in this book is set out in good
faith for general guidance and no liability can be accepted
for loss or expense incurred as a result of relying in particular
circumstances on statements made in the book. Laws and
regulations are complex and liable to change, and readers should
check the current position with the relevant authorities before
making personal arrangements.

Contents

Since the essential guidance for essay writing doesn't change from one level to another, I believe this book will benefit students from age 14 to MA level, with A-level the average pitch of the text. I have very much kept in mind the needs of mature students who have returned to formal studies after a period away from them, and students from overseas. Anyone in working life, who has to produce pieces of writing (from advertisements to business reports) that require basic planning and writing-up skills, should also find the book useful.

Essay writing can become a chore if you plunge in without clear objectives. It can become a joy, however, if you know how to select a topic that will keep you enthused, prepare well and master the other basic skills. Practise what this book proposes, and you will find increasing satisfaction with your essays, and the motivation to improve with each one.

Students' strategies for essay writing vary according to temperament and according to the subject. This book helps you to develop your own strategy. Find out what works for you and adapt the guidance to your own requirements.

A note on style. 'Quote' is used for extracts from speeches

or ordinary texts, 'quotations' for classic literary quotes.

I am indebted to the following organisations for permission to reproduce essay titles: ULEAC (University of London Examinations and Assessment Council), the Open University, Oxford Delegacy of Local Examinations and the Southern Examining Group.

Brendan Hennessy

Chapter 1

Embracing Your Topic

Commit yourself wholeheartedly to
producing what the topic requires.

It is worth giving time to:

◆ **understanding what the topic requires**

◆ **getting the question clear**

◆ **interpreting key terms and instructions**

◆ **paraphrasing the topic**

◆ **choosing the topic to live with**

Assuming you have a choice, the above considerations add up to giving the topics offered sufficient thought before deciding which to take on. If you choose one that for one reason or another doesn't suit you, you may be creating difficulties from the start. You may find yourself struggling with all the other stages in writing an essay covered in this book, because your heart won't be in it.

Even if only one topic is offered, plunging in without working out exactly what is wanted is dangerous: you will be tempted to concentrate on the aspect of the subject that immediately appeals to you rather than on what you are expected to concentrate on.

Choose the topic that you feel you can **do justice to**. That means not simply which topic you like most, or which topic you feel you know most about. Ask yourself if you are tempted to choose such topics because you feel you know most of the answers already or because you feel it will be easier to write about. Another topic might induce you to collect information more diligently. The result might be a more original essay that would satisfy better a tutor's or exam board's expectations.

Case study

I'm trying to get started on an essay entitled ' "The story is the tragedy of Okonkwo". In what ways do you find *Things That Fall Apart* a tragic novel?'

What does the phrase 'in what ways' mean? I mean it's one tragedy after another. Oknonkwo is a great man in his Ibo tribe in Nigeria. He has many great qualities but he's rooted in the past and doesn't agree with the way the tribe's culture is changing. This causes him several misfortunes, even before the white colonists arrive from the West. Then the tribe's way of life is changed and the society splits apart and Christianity brings hatred and turmoil as the society is conquered. Okonkwo is too rigid to change and the only solution for him is to commit suicide. This book is not a barrel of laughs.

To get back to my tragedy, I've got pages and pages of notes
and I'm only up to chapter 4. I seem to be rewriting the
whole book. I mean, there are so many sad things happening,
with Okonwo slapping his wives and children all over the place.

Understanding what the topic requires

The question on *Things Fall Apart* is apparently quite
straightforward. But **even the simplest question needs to be
interpreted.** The student faced with this essay hasn't
appreciated that **in what ways** means give **examples of the
key events and developments** in the novel which add up to a
tragedy, and it also means **explain the significance of the key
events and developments.** The length of essay asked for
dictates the number of events and developments you will
make a note of.

> The most common fault in essays is failure to answer
> the question. Read through the topics and be clear about
> their requirements before making a choice.

Note from the wording of the topic that two tragedies are
implied: the personal tragedy of Okonkwo and the tragedy
of his society covered by the novel. This is reflected in the
title, a quotation from W.B. Yeats's poem *The Second
Coming*, about a society torn apart by war. The next few
lines summarise Chinua Achebe's novel vividly and would be
worth quoting:

Things fall apart; the centre cannot hold;
Mere anarchy is loosed upon the world,
The blood-dimmed tide is loosed, and everywhere
The ceremony of innocence is drowned.

The student should be noting only the key aspects of character (with his beliefs and flaws) that prevent Okonkwo from changing, from living in the new world being created, and the key aspects (and beliefs) of a society whose 'innocence' is unequal to the new forces of disruption. He is proud, obstinate and prone to eruptions of anger; and the main events are his murder of a boy, his accidental killing of a friend's son, and his exile from his tribe.

Other topics, especially at GCSE level, are expressed as neat titles, without either instructional words or question. Supply instructional words when they are missing.

Consider, for example, 'Sunday morning'. This topic is **creative**, and it seems to leave you free to choose your content. Assume the missing instruction is **describe** or **give your memories of**. But beware. Your tutor will expect you to show some **imagination and writing skill**. Don't merely recount the main events of the day in chronological order or narrate events that could have happened on any ordinary day. Because it is a creative essay you would be expected to reflect on the significance of that particular Sunday morning in your life, humorous perhaps if not weighty.

Evoke your memories as vividly as possible. Bring to life the people who gathered round you on that day, and describe any noteworthy incident in an interesting, perhaps dramatic, way.

Other, more complex topics need to be interpreted very carefully. Take, for example: 'Argue the case against the banning of fox hunting'. If you're strongly against fox hunting, you may be delighted to find that term in an offered topic. You may be tempted to leap in and answer the wrong question: to argue the case **against** fox hunting. But the two negatives **against/banning** cancel each other out. Together they make a positive. The topic, in fact, requires you to argue for fox hunting.

Getting the question clear

Take care with three categories of topic:

◆ Where there is an implicit question, not expressed.

◆ Where the topic requires several sentences, or is built round a quote or quotation.

◆ Where there are underlying assumptions, which need to be recognised.

This history topic fits these three categories: 'People don't seem to realise that it takes time and effort and preparation to think. Statesmen are too busy making speeches to think.' Bertrand Russell. Discuss with reference to either Gladstone or Disraeli.

Clearly there is some truth in the quoted statement but it is not the whole truth. If you don't unravel the question behind the instruction **discuss**, the danger is that you may think you have been asked to find only evidence that supports the quote, ignoring the other side of the argument.

One way of dealing with a topic that contains a question that has not been expressed is to **turn the statement into a question**. In this case the question would be something like: 'How accurately do you think Russell's statement applies to the career of . . . ?'

> You should question the assumptions of a topic.

Note that a quote used as a basis for discussion does not need to be taken at face value. Isn't the way a statesman thinks, you might want to argue, as valid a way of thinking as the more philosophical kind? But an essay in history, not philosophy, is wanted. Here you could indicate your reservations about the quoted statement but go on to apply it as required.

Interpreting key terms and instructions

After reacting to topics as a whole, you need to look at elements more closely. They are of three kinds:

1. **Key terms or concepts.** These indicate what area of subject matter your essay should cover.

2. **Instructional words**. These tell you what to do with the subject-matter. Explain, argue, discuss and so on.

3. **Other pointers** to what is expected include such phrases as 'how far', 'in what ways'.

Before rushing into your essay, identify the key terms in your topic – underline them. **Key terms need to be defined.** For example: 'Argue the case against the <u>banning</u> of <u>corporal</u> <u>punishment</u> of <u>children</u> in <u>schools</u>.'

◆ **Banning,** in such a general context, may be defined as prohibited, made illegal.

◆ **Corporal punishment** needs more care. There is a wide range of corporal punishment, from a slap on the wrist to grievous bodily harm, and you will have to decide where you draw the line.

◆ **Children**. Then you realise it depends what you mean by children. How will the definition of 'corporal punishment' vary according to different ages of children? Should the criteria, moreover, be the same for parent, nanny, child-minder and teacher?

◆ **Schools**. Are you to consider primary, secondary, special needs?

You can see that by analysing the key terms of the topic in this way you may be formulating a **basic outline** for the essay.

> Meanings of key terms can vary according to context, subjects and disciplines.

Use your dictionary, of course, to help you define key terms, but note how much meanings can vary according to context. For example, consider how you would define 'banning' in this context: 'Do you agree to parents banning television until homework is completed?'

Note also how key terms vary in meaning according to subjects and disciplines. For most topics **poverty** will have a straightforward meaning, but for an essay in sociology you might have to take account of various definitions of the term employed by different theorists. You might have to indicate where they disagree, and where you stand.

If writing a literature essay based on a quotation, be careful to identify where a key term carries a contemporary meaning different from its current meaning. If you are asked to discuss, for example, Hamlet's 'Thus conscience does make cowards of us all' you will need to be aware that 'conscience' carries the meaning of 'knowledge' or 'awareness', not its current meaning.

It is also important to make sure you **interpret the instructions correctly**. The following is a list of instructional words that students occasionally misinterpret:

compare	find similarities and differences between
contrast	indicate the differences between
discuss	examine in detail, argue, give reasons for and against
describe	give a detailed account of
illustrate	explain with examples
refute	prove a statement/argument to be false.

Paraphrasing the topic

When you find it difficult to get your head round a topic, try putting it into your own words: **paraphrasing** it. Let's do this with 'Argue the case against the banning of fox hunting'. It could be paraphrased as: 'What are the arguments for keeping fox hunting legal?'

It's always advisable to check your paraphrase with your tutor or a fellow-student: if it's incorrect, your essay will go off the rails. Suppose you came up with the following effort at paraphrase: 'Do you think fox hunting should remain legal?' Your resulting essay might express your views clearly and persuasively. Unfortunately, it's one side of the argument that is required, not (except incidentally) your views.

Choosing the topic to live with

The title of this chapter uses the word **embracing** to emphasise **the need for commitment** to the topic you choose, especially for a term essay. You must feel that you will maintain interest in the topic for the period alloted. You must feel that the energy and enthusiasm required for research will not flag. You must also feel that your chosen topic will allow you to do justice to the abilities you possess, which the essay has been designed to test. In general terms, essays test that you can:

◆ collect information quickly and use the knowledge to focus clearly on the set topic

◆ read critically and purposefully

◆ analyse processes and problems and argue a case

◆ relate theory to specific examples

◆ make a creative (original) contribution to the subject

◆ structure the material logically, express it clearly and present it in the format expected.

There may also be specific requirements for your essay, which your tutor will advise you of.

> Remember: embracing a topic means keeping it constantly in view.

If you don't keep a topic constantly in view you will waste time studying and noting the irrelevant, and you will digress when writing up. You can keep it in view by:

◆ putting the title on a card and displaying it above or on your desk.

◆ writing the title as a heading to your work at every stage – notes, plan, first draft, final version.

Practice

(After completing these exercises, check with the Responses in Appendix A, page 85.)

1. 'Sunday morning' lacked an instructional word and we supplied 'describe' or 'give your memories of'. Add a short sentence or two to the following titles in order to suggest how they should be treated:

   (a) 'My favourite restaurant'
   (b) 'If I were Prime Minister'
   (c) 'Friendship'

2. Turn the following topic into a question: 'Refute the arguments that are made in favour of caring for the mentally ill in the community'.

3. Underline the key terms in the following topics:

   (a) Do you approve of competition in schools?

   (b) 'Celebrities have a right to a private life'. Discuss

   (c) How important is the Fool's role in *King Lear*?

4. Paraphrase each of the topics of exercise 3, supplying suitable instructional terms where not stated.

Chapter 2

Taking Notes

A good note-taking system will help you to produce accurate and relevant information from the start.

Here is a system that works well for essays:

◆ **working to a timetable**

◆ **noting ideas**

◆ **noting facts and opinions**

◆ **ordering your notes**

◆ **paraphrasing, summarising and recalling**

Avoid taking too many notes, which will make it hard to see a pattern to follow. Avoid taking too few: you may run out of ideas half way through the writing. Take the right amount of notes by **keeping their purposes** constantly in mind.

The three purposes of note-taking are:

◆ **To stimulate your own thinking** on the subject so that there is some originality in your viewpoint or argument. At all stages of note-taking, jot down your own reactions.

◆ **To collect information accurately,** in the form of ideas, opinions and facts. Check one source against another, depending on the time available.

◆ **To collect relevant information.** Take a little more than you need, and select the most useful. Relate your research to the topic you are covering by writing the topic at the head of all sections of notes, drafts, etc.

Working to a timetable

A short essay (say up to 500 words on 'The street or road I live in') may be written out of your head and may need only one draft. Any topic requiring greater length and complexity has to be done in stages. **Make a timetable,** working back from the date of the **final version deadline,** showing when you should have completed:

◆ notes of your immediate reactions to the topic

◆ survey of the sources of information suggested (course outline, reading lists, companies/individuals to interview)

◆ research of your subject area and topic

◆ one or two essay plans

◆ first draft

◆ final version deadline.

Noting ideas

Aim for some originality from the start. Consider the topic: 'What examples of sexism can you find in this country today?' Here is a useful plan of action:

◆ Note what ideas you already have on the topic.

◆ Test your own ideas against those of others.

◆ Stimulate your thinking by brainstorming.

> The simplest brainstorming method is formulating some of the questions that an analysis of the topic provides. One question will suggest another.

Example

(Concise Oxford Dictionary definition: 'prejudice, stereotyping, or discrimination, typically against women, on the basis of sex'.)

1 What are the typical manifestations of sexism?

2 What special contributions can males make to: ideas, problem solving, various jobs, other aspects of life?

3 What special contributions can females make to these aspects?

4 How far are the female contributions being recognised?

5 Where does ageism combine with sexism to create further impediments (acting seems an obvious example)?

6 In what kinds of employment is sexism most prevalent? The professions? (Contrast the roles/status of men and women in, for example, the law, the church, the armed forces, journalism.)

7 In what areas of life/employment are men treated unfairly on the grounds of their sex?

8 What recourse to the law do victims of sexism have? How effective are the safeguards? Is the control over sexist adverts effective? (Talk to the Advertising Standards Authority.)

Initial ideas can be put into the form of a **mind map®**, in question or statement form, especially if you have quite a lot of ideas in your head at the start and you want to look at them and play about with them immediately. A mind map used at the planning stage is illustrated on page 26. You now know what you are looking for and can begin to research your topic at greater depth. The essential research skills are as follows.

Noting facts and opinions

Whichever sources of information you use, learn to distinguish between facts and opinions — those in your sources, and your own facts and opinions.

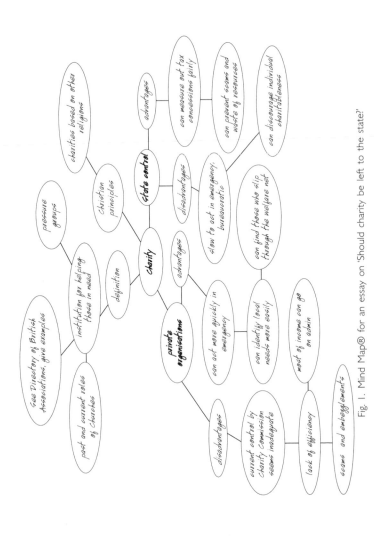

Fig. 1. Mind Map® for an essay on 'Should charity be left to the state?'

Call your note taking gathering information, or if it is sufficiently ambitious call it research. Whichever, there are five sources:

1 from personal knowledge and experience

2 by legwork

3 by interview

4 from the print media (books and publications) and the Internet – called library research for convenience

5 from the broadcast media (radio and television)

6 from film (cinema and video).

You may need only one of these sources for a straightforward essay of about a thousand words. For a fairly complicated coursework project you may want to use several.

Personal knowledge and experience

The creative essay ('My Sundays', 'Nightmares') may demand no more than what is in your head (and heart). In other kinds of essay you will be combining your personal knowledge and experience with what you can find out.

When tackling subjects where what's in your head can only be part of the answer ('What are the effects of TV on family life – positive and negative?') you will want to compare your own experiences with those of others and perhaps with surveys and other printed information. You will recognise that examiners will expect you to go beyond individual expression to develop some thoughtful, general conclusions.

On the whole, recognise that for essays requiring some kind of research, it's what you find out that's interesting rather than what you happen to know.

Legwork

This is the newspaper reporter's term for going out and finding out for yourself. You would probably base an essay describing your street, the local leisure centre, supermarket, favourite restaurant or art exhibition on notes taken during a visit rather than depending on your memory (assuming that you've been given time).

Interview

An essay project (for example, on anorexia) may require you to be up to date on the subject. Even the most recent book on the subject, if published in the past few months, was probably written a year or more ago. Find out what's been published recently in newspapers and magazines, then armed with your notes and questions, find an expert to interview.

An anorexic, if you can contact one, is one kind of expert. You may find a GP or nurse specialising in the problem. Consult the Directory of British Associations to find out which association or society deals with anorexia (librarians will guide you in this). You may be able to interview an expert office-holder of the society, and gather some literature about their activities.

Library research

Know how to use a library. Get to know a reference library intimately and use it regularly, including the computerised databases. Acquaint yourself with the indexes that list articles published in newspapers and magazines, and with directories that list details of organisations (such as Age Concern) that would supply you with literature about subjects you are studying (such as ageism) and may agree to be interviewed. The librarian will always help.

A gateway site on the Internet guides you to relevant and reliable information on a particular subject.

Sample books to judge their usefulness. How relevant to your topic is a particular book or article? Note for example:

- the qualifications of the author

- the date of publication

- the contents page and main headings

- the index

- the preface or introduction

Read books at the level they demand: skim, scan or read in depth:

Skimming means quickly exploring the ground, noting what will be useful for your purposes.

Scanning means that you search out exactly what you want, ignoring the rest.

In depth means that you read the relevant parts, questioning critically.

Broadcast media and film

When working on an essay project, consult listings to see if there are any radio or TV documentaries, or films about to be shown that relate to your subject. Organisations that need to keep the public informed of their progress often supply videos as well as literature.

> To back up your viewpoint, you are just as interested in opinions for evidence as in facts. But it is authoritative opinions that you are interested in: that is, opinions based on facts.

Strongly based views may be based on lack of knowledge or misunderstandings. An elderly interviewee, for instance, may believe that he was turned down for a new post on the grounds of age. Further research may reveal that the company decided to distribute the new tasks among existing posts rather than create a new post.

Your supportive material will be enlivened by **anecdotal evidence**, that is stories and case studies, and by **illustrative**

examples and **analogies** that make your discussion clear.
Indicate the sources for your notes. At the writing up stage
you may need to refer back to the sources to check that you
have noted them accurately, or to quote from them,
indicating how far you agree with them. It is a good idea to
put your own reactions to what you are noting in square
brackets [ ] as you go, so that you can easily see at writing
up stage where you stand, and the pattern that your
discussion is likely to take.

Do not assume that any fact is correct, however renowned
the author, or that any opinion is valid, however
authoritative, or that any anecdote has been remembered
clearly. Many errors creep into books and newspapers.
Check one source against the other when there is doubt, and
you have the time to do so.

In practice you will be expected to base your discussion
on a balance of reasonable evidence. You will save time
by carefully selecting reliable sources from the start.

Ordering your notes

Use whichever arrangement or combination of arrangements
suit you best for particular projects. Make sure you indicate
sources and prepare a separate **bibliography** if you refer to
several books and articles. Recommended arrangements are:

◆ a simple folder

- a loose-leaf ring binder
- note cards

You may want to combine one or two systems.

1. **A simple folder.** For an essay up to 1,000 words a simple folder may be sufficient, to contain perhaps lecture notes, notes from a book or two, and from a few articles, and photocopied newspaper cuttings and leaflets with the main points highlighted. You may also have pencilled notes in books of your own (not to be done in library books). Ideally, select the most relevant notes and transfer them to A4 sheets, with a new sheet for each aspect of your topic, writing on one side of the paper only.

2. **A loose-leaf ring binder.** For lengthier projects requiring more notes and materials. Use dividers to separate different aspects.

3. **6" x 4" note cards.** They can easily be ordered by shuffling. Cards encourage you to be concise and to paraphrase rather than copy slavishly.

4. **5" x 3" bibliography cards.** Shuffle them into alphabetical order as you go, and you have an ordered bibliography to copy at the finish. Cards are illustrated on the opposite page.

Case study

I'm not very good at taking notes at class lectures and I miss important points. If I borrow a friend's notes afterwards I can't

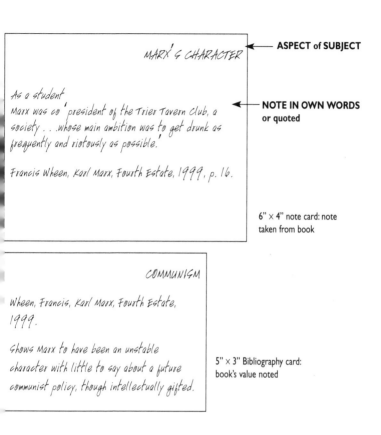

MARX'S CHARACTER — **ASPECT of SUBJECT**

As a student
Marx was co 'president of the Trier Tavern Club, a
society . . .whose main ambition was to get drunk as
frequently and riotously as possible.'

Francis Wheen, Karl Marx, Fourth Estate, 1999, p. 16.

— **NOTE IN OWN WORDS**
or quoted

6" × 4" note card: note
taken from book

COMMUNISM

Wheen, Francis, Karl Marx, Fourth Estate,
1999.

Shows Marx to have been an unstable
character with little to say about a future
communist policy, though intellectually gifted.

5" × 3" Bibliography card:
book's value noted

Fig. 2. Note cards

read their writing or I can't decipher their system of
abbreviation or I can't work out their thought processes. Once
I start reading the necessary books or articles I become so
fascinated by the subject I read much more than I need to,
following all the interesting byways of the subject, and I take far
too many notes. I then have a terrible job selecting what is

relevant and putting it in order. I am generally late submitting my assignments.

An ancient Tibetan proverb says, 'Either you eat life or it eats you'. The more information you collect the more difficult it is to select the significant and find your way to your own ideas.

The following procedure will make your tasks easier:

Paraphasing, summarising and recalling

1. **Take notes in your own words.** Paraphrasing will ensure that you will end up with an original approach to the subject and not merely a re-hash of others' views, without any ideas of your own. Passages used as evidence must be enclosed within quotes. There should not be too many quoted passages and they must be integrated into your essay by having their relevance to the topic commented on.

2. **Summarise to avoid taking too many notes.** As with paraphrasing, you are using your own words and putting your own stamp on the material.

3. **Use an abbreviation system:** e.g. 'Prepg essay, gd note takg systm = accte relt info.

4. **Oral recall.** Get a fellow-student to question you on your notes or texts. Note any lapses in your responses.

5. **Written recall.** Study any important section of your notes or texts, put it aside and write a summary of the main points. Then check.

6. Review. Read through all your notes, checking against the texts for accuracy, filling in any observable gaps.

Practice

1. You are writing an essay about organic food and need to make a brief reference to the increased demand. Note two important points as far as possible in your own words (not more than 20 words for each point) from this extract from the article 'Planet Organic' (*The Observer Magazine*, 27 June 1999). Assume that the information is up to date.

> Anyone who has stepped into a supermarket recently will be aware of the explosion in demand for organic food. Waitrose and Sainsbury's now stock more than 400 organic lines, and their rivals are making strenuous efforts to catch up, while organic restaurants, cafés, juice bars and greengrocers are springing up in urban high streets. At the moment, 70 per cent of organic produce is being imported: domestic farmers and growers can't keep up with demand, although, for the first time in history, more land is now in conversion (a process that takes about three years) than in production, and the Soil Association reckons that it receives 40 calls a day from farmers eager to make the switch.

2 Continue practising the art of precis as indicated above, to provide notes for your essays or to provide notes for revision in various subjects.

Chapter 3

Finding the Best Plan

Planning helps you to think fruitfully, to discover what you want to say and to see how to put it into a coherent shape.

You can also be creative while:

- **using brainstorming techniques**
- **selecting the controlling idea**
- **matching plans to topics**

Thoughts, as they come to us, are rarely in coherent order. Listen to a conversation or even a tape-recorded interview and the best of thinkers ramble and repeat themselves. You may, nevertheless, find that you think more fruitfully in the act of writing. You like, perhaps, to jot down a few main points and dive into a rough draft, leaving the re-ordering and planning until later. For most essays, however, you will need to impose order at an early stage by planning.

There are two kinds of plan:

- **brainstorming,** generally a creative, informal kind

- **linear-logical,** or **formal.**

Experiment to discover the kind of planning that best suits

you and your topic. We start with the informal kind, because it is especially useful at the early, idea-forming stage. It can be used at any later stage too, when you are at an impasse.

Case study

What a topic to throw at you for the Easter holidays: 'What is the evidence that suggests that watching much television can be damaging?' I'm bothered, bewildered and gobsmacked. It's too obvious isn't it? It makes you passive, and all the dumbed down stuff, chewing gum for the eyes, can't be good for the brain. Well, I've said it. What more do they want? I try to make a plan and find I've got nothing to put in it. So then I try to think up more ideas so that a plan will suggest itself. But they don't come: I know what I want to say in a nutshell, but that doesn't make an essay.

Evidence doesn't come out of the top of your head. You need to look for it and think about it, then assess it. The emphasis in this title is on collecting the evidence (by implication both for and against) and on showing what evidence has to be considered rather than making judgements.

If you find yourself responding to a topic with 'It's obvious, isn't it?' reflect that if it were obvious you wouldn't have been asked the question. Most topics require you to look for facts and ideas. A mind map might get the ideas flowing. Facts will have to be gathered on such a subject: depending on the time available, some reading into the subject (magazine articles?, newspaper articles?, is there a book on the subject?) will be needed. To interpret the facts, to assess their significance, some discussion with members of your family and friends will help.

When you find you quickly come to a halt when trying to gather ideas, first ask yourself whether you read enough, and secondly try different methods of brainstorming.

Using brainstorming techniques

Brainstorming means experimenting with word and idea associations. The various techniques help you to discover fresh ideas. We have seen the simplest technique in operation: formulating questions and letting one question (or answer) suggest another (see pages 24–25). Here are other brainstorming techniques:

◆ The five Ws plus how.

◆ People and Perspectives.

◆ Mind maps®.

Five Ws plus how. Newspaper reporters are programmed to collect evidence by asking who, what, where, when, why and how? The essay writer can often work in the same way. Let's associate those questions with a topic and see how we would group the evidence. 'What is the evidence that suggests that watching too much television can be damaging?'

◆ Who: affecting whom – young child, college student, housewife or househusband?

◆ What: dangers of increasing passivity, of reducing attention span, of killing conversation.

◆ Where: TV sets in different rooms of a house.

◆ When: How many hours of the day?

◆ Why: arguments, for example, based on the way television tends to provide answers rather than ask questions.

◆ How: TV watching becomes addictive, unselective, 'chewing gum for the eyes'.

History, politics and sociology essays benefit from this approach.

Some topics are best served by a version of the above technique, called **People and Perspectives**. Confronted with 'Why did Henry II quarrel with Thomas Becket, Archbishop of Canterbury?' you may be full of facts but unable to see a path through them. The order of the names implies that the perspective of the king is wanted. Clearly the **attitude** of the king to Becket's defending the rights of the Church against those of the monarchy needs to be covered. The psychological facts as well as the constitutional facts are needed. One you've studied the period, put yourself into the king's place and imagine how he felt about Becket. You can now see a way of ordering and shaping your ideas.

If you have time, you may want to read a play about Becket, for example T.S. Eliot's *Murder in the Cathedral* or a more recent one, and set its theme alongside the historical facts.

Mind maps®. The main advantage of mind maps (also called mind webs, concept trees and 'spiders') is that they encourage lateral thinking. This means thinking sideways, illogically, unpredictably, with the aim of finding fresh approaches and ideas for a topic. Study the mind map on page 26 for the topic 'Should charity be left to the state?' You follow one aspect out from the middle of a page. Then because you can see them all at once, as you see a landscape from an aeroplane, you see other connections sideways that you wouldn't see with a logical scheme, which is more like seeing the landscape from a train.

Selecting the controlling idea

A controlling idea is needed to give an essay unity and coherence. That idea, depending on the topic, might be more appropriately called a viewpoint, a thesis, a theme or an explanation.

You may find it hard to write without a plan. Or you may find the more interesting ideas come to you in the course of writing.

A short essay will have a controlling idea imposed early on (prisons should be fewer/ fewer people should be imprisoned/ more prisons should be built).

> If you find a controlling idea soon after researching, you will find it easier to avoid digressing and taking too many notes.

Keep in mind the **basic outline**:

◆ introduction, or beginning

◆ body, or middle

◆ conclusion, or ending.

Matching plans to topics

There are simple and detailed versions of the logical plan. The simple version is building points into paragraphs. A straightforwardly narrative or decriptive essay requiring little exposition or argument can be planned with a list of points.

Take, for example 'My local leisure centre'. The points might be: the building and its setting, the layout indicating the various facilities, the pool or pools, the various facilities at the pools (diving boards, chutes, waves, etc), other attractions for children, facilities for other sports (gymnasium, squash, etc), sauna, cafeteria or restaurant.

Five hundred words might be divided as: 60 words for an introductory paragraph, 40 words for the conclusion, and about 50 words for each of the eight paragraphs of the body.

The points may be expressed in a **statement-per-paragraph** plan, a particularly useful form for a simple argument such as: 'Parents should bear more responsibility for the crimes of their children'.

For an essay largely in agreement with the proposition the statements would no doubt include:

- The quality of parental guidance seems to be deteriorating.
- <u>But</u> punishing parents (eg by fining) only destabilises the family further.
- Schools have to bear too much of the blame.
- The police cannot be expected to do more monitoring of young delinquents.

Underline any links that come to you when ordering points, as with 'But' above.

At an earlier stage of a project, or for an essay that is going to be less sure of its position, the points may be arranged in a question-per-paragraph plan:

- Is the quality of parental guidance deteriorating? . . . and so on.

For the more 'creative' kind of essay ('Earliest Memories') you may prefer to think up ideas as you go, and write a few drafts.

For longer projects, where the notes are fairly numerous, a **detailed formal plan** will be most convenient. An example with some linking indicated, is given for the title 'Should charity be left to the state?' in Appendix B.

Test your plan before writing up:

1. Is there a unified theme?

2. Is every point relevant and well connected?

3. Do the title, introduction and conclusion chime, as a team, making it clear what the viewpoint is?

Practice

1. Make a question-per-paragraph plan for the topic 'What may be the effects of an increase in leisure time?' (GCSE Sociology, June 1993, ULEAC.)

2. Make a list of four or five points for the TV Damage topic. Do a little brainstorming and research first. After each point, put the possible benefit of this aspect (starting with 'But'), so that in the course of the essay you would be able to anticipate reservations that readers might raise. Consider different kinds of programmes. A first pair of points is supplied:

   Evidence of TV damage
   Everything is shown on TV so that you tend to take it all in passively. It doesn't encourage you to think. For

example, watching a TV adaptation of a great novel you are not encouraged to come to your own conclusions about the author, the characters or the issues raised.

But
A TV adaptation can bring the book to life, make you see exactly how people lived, what clothes they wore, etc. It can take you enthusiastically to the book.

Chapter 4

Beginning and Ending

Begin with a promise that attracts interest.
End by showing that you have fulfilled your promise.

The essential principles are:

◆ **introducing with a promise**

◆ **arousing interest and curiosity**

◆ **summing up at the end**

◆ **finalising the question**

◆ **leaving something to think about**

The beginning (introduction) and ending (conclusion) add up to **about a third of the essay.** The ending is usually a little shorter than the beginning.

They are usually the most difficult parts to write, but attempt them in the first draft to keep yourself on track. Rewrite them after the body is done, when you realise what you have actually said.

Much can be learnt from studying the beginnings and endings of newspaper features and magazine articles.

Broadsheet ones are closer to the academic essay and don't tend to sacrifice substance to style or entertainment, as the tabloid features can. Tabloid features, however, can teach us a lot about how to attract attention.

Fulfilling the promise of an essay means **establishing your viewpoint.** You will have explained or argued with conviction, and you will have persuaded the reader at least to think about what you had to say.

Introducing with a promise

The beginning, or introduction, has to be a link between the title and the essay. It must indicate, either explicitly or implicitly:

◆ what the topic means

◆ how you intend to limit the subject.

The start of an essay by Graham Greene, the novelist, called 'The Lost Childhood', does these things subtly and concisely:

> Perhaps it is only in childhood that books have any deep influence on our lives. In later life we admire, we are entertained, we may modify some views we already hold, but we are more likely to find in books merely a confirmation of what is in our minds already: as in a love affair it is our own features that we see reflected flatteringly back.

Where the viewpoint is more tentative, or the topic is complex, as in 'Is the work ethic outdated?', the writer may choose to take the reader by the hand and give a slightly more detailed idea of the plan to be followed. It might run like this:

> I shall show how the work ethic has developed through history . . . its association with (as examples) Christian and Muslim principles . . . compare the force of the work ethic in present-day Christian and Muslim states . . . the role of government . . . the role of the media . . .

When you signpost the order of well-defined sections in this way you must of course keep to that order in the body of the essay. You will have made it easier for yourself to make the transitions from one section to the next: the reader is anticipating you. The reader will not prefer the essay to have had more impact, more liveliness, if it would have been at the expense of clarity.

Clarity is the most important quality of an essay.

Case study

I tend to write boring beginnings and endings. The beginnings explain what the title means and what I am aiming to do. They are usually clear, but I don't seem to be able to make them readable. Then, although the body of the essay may be well structured I don't see how to round it off. I feel I've covered the ground so that there's no more left to say. The essay comes to a sudden stop, and it reads as though I've run out of ideas.

Arousing interest and curiosity

Whether you are indicating viewpoint or signposting what is to come, aim to **arouse interest** at the same time. It will sharpen attention for what you have to say. Ways of arousing interest are:

1. **Move from abstract to concrete.** You could begin an essay by saying that during the Second World War airmen came into a hospital badly injured. Or you could immediately make it concrete, to let the reader see it. You could, for example, tell an anecdote or relate a startling fact or statistic. An article in *The Mail on Sunday* begins:

   There were four ways in which airmen used to come into Ward 3 of the Queen Victoria Hospital in East Grinstead during the war: boiled, mashed, fried and roast. 'Just like potatoes really', said one of them.

2. **Use a quotation or a quote.** A student's essay on 'What is education for?' begins:

   I think the 19th century philosopher Herbert Spencer expressed it best, certainly most concisely. He said, 'Education has for its object the formation of character' ... I believe its purpose is, or should be, to help us to develop the character and skills to live at peace and earn our living in the society we find ourselves in. I believe the key quality to acquire for this is balance.

Note that in a subtle way the student is both defining the key term 'character' and updating the associations.

There are numerous books of quotations, from both classical and modern authors. Make sure the quotation you choose is **relevant**, and no more than one (at the most two) per essay is advised in general. Essays on literature, of course, may demand many quotations and often quotes (e.g., from critics and commentators) as well.

What is said in a quote is usually more important than **who** said it. Experts will be quoted to add authority. Celebrities are often used for quotes in newspapers because they are a convenient shorthand for getting across the context. Writing about ageism, an article in *Ms London* magazine begins:

> 'You can be a 50-year-old anything except a 50-year-old actress,' Faye Dunaway said recently with some bitterness. In truth, ageism is a form of discrimination that doesn't only affect thespians and doesn't only affect 50-year-olds. Age discrimination in employment can affect everyone.

Notice how briskly the relevance of the quote is established by the viewpoint.

3. **Make the reader laugh or cry.** The quote about the airmen is enough to make you cry. Humour or wit is a wonderful way of making a point memorable if you can avoid relating a joke for its own sake because you believe

it's a good one rather than for its appropriateness to your theme. There are books of humorous quotations; you can ransack the great humorists of the past for yourself; you can note how it's done in weeklies such as *Private Eye* and *The Spectator*, and in newspapers and magazines that print humorous essays and personal columns and you can be funny on your own account.

Summing up at the end

Summing up means showing how the main points of the essay add up to an explanation, opinion, judgement or proof; showing that they add up to more than the sum of the parts.

Example
That previously quoted student's workmanlike essay on education ends:

> More immediately, education is vocational, to help students to pass exams and to prepare for careers that will suit their talents and special interests. But I have made the larger purposes the subject of this essay, because if there were no working towards them there would soon not be a world left to have a career in.

You want the conclusion to be memorable, and like the introduction it might need several drafts. Again, a quote, or a quotation or an anecdote might add vividness to an ending, but don't have one of these both at start and finish.

Finalising the question

There will be a definite viewpoint: now you know, the reader is told, why I began as I did. There is a kind of echo to the beginning. There may be a final answer to a question raised at the beginning, or some kind of solution to a problem raised there. Joan Didion, the American writer, brings the rhythms and resonance of poetry into the satisfying conclusion to her essay 'On Morality' (quoted in Thomas S. Kane's *The New Oxford Guide to Writing*):

> Because when we start deceiving ourselves into thinking not that we want something or need something, not that it is a pragmatic necessity for us to have it, but that it is a moral imperative that we have it, that is when we join the fashionable madmen, and then is when the thin whine of hysteria is heard in the land, and then is when we are in bad trouble. And I think we are already there.

An extra long sentence or an extra short one, or one followed by the other as here, makes for a strong ending.

> The conclusion should clinch the matter, there should be a satisfying finality about it.

A **fake conclusion** is easily recognised. Essay writers sometimes try to suggest in their conclusions that they have presented a reasonable argument, or have provided clinching evidence, hoping that some stylish writing will cover up the inadequacy of their attempts. **But it won't.**

Leaving something to think about

When the conclusion is tentative, it may appear in the form of a question or an implied judgement, rather than a restatement of a thesis. Joan Didion's 'I think' in the above example shows how to follow conviction with speculation about the future.

In any case, if dealing with an ongoing problem you may want to build up to a new perspective on the topic, give the reader a new question to think about, that will need to draw on the evidence or argument you have provided.

Practice

- ◆ Give your own introduction for the essay 'How, do you think, should education prepare us for life?' Find a different quotation, or anecdote, to get you started.
- ◆ Then write a brief outline for the body.
- ◆ Then write a conclusion, including in it a look into the future.
- ◆ Get some feedback.

Chapter 5

Putting the Middle Together

*You know where you started from
and you know your destination.
Choose the best route.*

This chapter gives you the techniques for:

◆ keeping to the point

◆ narrating in readable order

◆ describing precisely

◆ explaining fully

◆ arguing persuasively

If you succeed in these your essay will:

◆ flow, unified and coherent, with one controlling idea and
  with points logically connected

◆ reveal a strong desire to communicate, to share your
  interest in the topic with your readers.

Getting bogged down in notes or following a plan too
rigidly can deaden your interest and weaken your desire to
communicate. Conversely, an irritating, shapeless essay can
result from neglecting to order. **Experiment with different**

methods of writing up to see which works best for you.

It is usually best to concentrate on being **interesting** (sometimes passionate) in your first draft. Leave the finer points of style until the second.

Tear up false starts, rewrite plans that don't work and start again. You can refer back to the plan or the notes to see if anything important has been left out.

Case study

In my plans, and even in my first drafts, I tend to have one thing after another without connection. Sometimes it's because I have too many ideas and I haven't decided exactly what they add up to, what the unifying theme is. For example, in an essay entitled 'If I were Prime Minister' I tried to cover so many aspects of life today that it became just a catalogue of ideas.

Having been criticised for this several times, I now tend to sprinkle my final version with faked connectives – 'therefore', 'however', and such phrases as 'on the other hand' and 'having said that . . .' which don't fit the bill.

Keeping to the point

To repeat: **keep the topic in front of you at all stages,** at the head of your notes, of your plan, your drafts, even on a card pinned up in front of your desk. It is good to collect too many ideas, as long as you then reduce them to a manageable number that relate directly to the theme.

> Be as simple and direct as the subject allows.

Because the way your thoughts are connected is clearer to you than the reader you may fail to supply enough **connectives**. It is a failure of leadership: you must **guide your readers** through a journey that you have just made on your own, and you must anticipate what kind of guidance they need.

Techniques for connecting well are:

◆ Using conjunctions and conjunctival phrases: and, but, however, so, for example . . . Go easy on the 'ands' and 'buts'.

◆ **Using key terms.** In the charities article outlined on pages 91–93, key terms (and synonyms and near-synonyms of these) would make a network through the article and might include: charity, good causes, benefits, Lottery, largesse, grants, funds, schemes, scams, money, sponsorship, contributions, distributors, bureaucratic waste, corruption, morality, materialism, collectors, recipients, deserving, undeserving, disadvantaged . . .

◆ **Signposting.** You link up by referring to statements already made. In effect, you are saying: the foregoing has covered that, the following will cover this. Simple signposting uses pronouns, demonstratives, definite articles and comparative words (he, she, it, this, that,

those, the, similar, bigger . . .). Heavier signposting is
sometimes needed when a new paragraph changes gear.

◆ **Summarising link.** You summarise the topic of the last
paragraph and then, in the main clause, state the new
topic. Take, for example section I, 4 of the charities essay.
That could be a paragraph beginning: 'To set against this
asessment of the Lottery's contribution [point 3], let's
analyse the pros and cons in general of the way charities
operate [point 4 introduced].'

Parallelism. Within a paragraph, and from paragraph to
paragraph, parellelism makes the structure clear, helping
the reader to anticipate what's coming next. Here are
some phrases that might steer the reader smoothly
through a paragraph or (if the scope is larger) from one
paragraph to the next: 'Charities in Elizabethan times . . .
Victorian times . . . before the Lottery . . . since the
Lottery . . .'

Narrating in readable order

In an essay you are generally **narrating facts** as well as
events in response to such instructions as *relate, state* and
trace. An essay is unlikely to be pure narration, but parts of
a literature or history essay may have to concentrate on
telling the story. The narration may be mingled with the
exposition (analysing and explaining), might follow the
charting of events.

Examples of topics requiring you to tell the story and explain are:

'Relate the procedure for carrying out a scientific experiment, or for a gardening task, or for organising a party.'

'State the main events that led to the Crimean War.'

'Trace the development of Celie's character from an oppressed teenager to an independent woman through *The Colour Purple*'.

Narrative technique depends on choosing the most effective order for the purpose.

◆ **Chronological order** suggests itself for simple narration of events, although you may want to vary it by plunging into the story at a dramatic point to grab the reader's interest, filling in the earlier part later. This borrowing of techniques from fiction is common in feature articles but must be done sparingly in essays.

◆ **Climax order,** the storyteller's main trick, keeps the reader in suspenseful interest (what happened next?) and can be used in essays when appropriate. There, however, the drama is likely to be modified into least important to most important, or unfamiliar to familiar.

◆ Clarity sometimes demands the **anti-climax order,** from the familiar to the unfamiliar. You might show the effects of a disease or an accident first, so that the causes will be understood.

Literature topics apparently asking for narration but requiring something more complex have to be interpreted with care. The *Colour Purple* topic above requires more than the sequence of events.

'But where do you start?' the student asks. 'Celie is developing all the time. The whole novel is about her developing.'

What the essay needs to identify here are Celie's **crisis** points. These are where there are crucial changes — highly significant stages in her development. With this understanding, the student is unlikely to be overwhelmed by too many notes. Having identified Celie's crisis points, the student will find it easy to fill in the explanation: will be able to explain **who** and **what** help her to develop at each point, and what the new Celies have become at each point. The essay would include, as some comment on those crisis points, how the author achieves the effects aimed at.

Compare the comments made about *Things That Fall Apart* on pages 13–14. A similar approach is required by 'Identify the events in Charlotte Brontë's *Jane Eyre* that serve to mould the heroine's character'.

Describing precisely

The instructional word **describe** is used in two rather different senses:

◆ paint a word picture of

◆ give a detailed account of, discuss.

Responding to the instruction in its first sense, as in 'Describe the street or road you live in as precisely as you can' your aim would be to make readers **feel they are there.** You would make them see it, touch it, hear it, smell it and taste it.

'Describe the procedures of a typical GPs' practice' has the instruction in the second sense. Your aim would be to help readers understand a logical sequence of events and some explanation of the way the business is managed. If a lengthy essay requiring much discussion is wanted, the instruction may be **describe and explain.**

The two tasks are more difficult to do well than that little word 'describe' suggests. They both need you to use **powers of observation and imagination.**

◆ Develop your **powers of observation** by going for a walk, keeping your eyes open, writing about what you saw on your return, and later checking to see what you missed.

◆ Develop your **imagination** by reading the best literature and enlivening your responses to it and to your experiences.

The first topic reminds us that the crucial quality in choice of words is **precision** (more about that in Chapter 6). Not only precise words, but **words in the right order** are demanded. That means the best order for the purpose. In descriptions the best order may be chronological, as in 'Describe a landscape from a moving train'. The best order may be space order, as in describing a town with 'to the north... to the south... in the middle...' Or it may be a combination of these orders.

Explaining fully

To explain, the dictionary tells us, means 'to make something clear by describing it in more detail' or 'give a reason or justification for'. Look again at the definitions given on pages 18–19. Note the shades of meaning between the various synonyms and near-synonyms used as instructional words: *analyse, define, clarify, compare, contrast, assess, illustrate.* Use a dictionary to help you interpret an instructional word.

The essay that explains is called an exposition. The essential qualities of the essay asked for are clarity, comprehensiveness and logical order.

The basic job is **analyse**: these are different parts or concepts covered by the subject: this is what they are, this is how they connect, and this is what they add up to.
Such a topic as 'Explain how Parliament works' may lead

you to describe the parts in something like this order:

1 the House of Commons and the House of Lords
2 who become Members and how
3 what their duties are
4 the roles of party leaders
5 the roles of Prime Minister and cabinet ministers
6 the role of the Civil Service

It's a logical order, but of course there are other logical orders. You might prefer, for example, to deal with number 2, later in the list. The important thing is that your account is coherent, clearly connected, making a picture that is easily understood.

Many expository essays require you to **define terms**. That is, say what it is. Correct misconceptions. Say what it isn't.

Careful definition is necessary when words vary in different disciplines. *Tragedy* and *comedy* as literary terms have meanings rather different from common usage. You may have to make it clear when using such words as *contempt* and *prejudice* whether you are using them in a legal sense or not. In psychology *response* and *stimulation* have specific jargon meanings.

To **illustrate** means to show with examples, to turn abstract into concrete. The numbers of people who died or who were made homeless will show how disastrous an earthquake was. An anecdote about how Napoleon dealt with his piles will give an insight into how he ruled France. Analogies (extended comparisons) are particularly useful to illustrate a subject that is complex or technical. The hidden, unfamiliar workings of the human body may be likened to the workings of familiar machines.

> Readers must feel that you are authoritative: the exposition must be knowledgeable, accurate and complete.

If one error is spotted readers will not be able to trust the truth of anything else you say. On a simple level, explaining how to cook chips could result in a house on fire if an important instruction is omitted.

Arguing persuasively

As with an exposition, you generally have to **prepare the ground by analysis** before setting out an argument. For example, you will probably have to **define terms, clarify issues,** or **remove misconceptions,** or all three. Tackling the topic 'Should corporal punishment be banned in schools?' will require fixing where you take corporal punishment to begin, at a gentle slap or at a hard one? You might want to distinguish between primary and secondary schools, and you might want to allow some punishment in one but not in the other.

There are three essential qualities in sound argument:

1. **Clear reasoning,** using such techniques as induction —

arguing from the particular to the general, deduction —
from the general to the particular, and avoiding fallacies.

2. **Cool weighing of the evidence** of facts and
opinions.

3. **Well-considered conclusions,** clearly based on the
evidence.

Case study

In a class discussion on pizza restaurants I stated categorically
that Pizza Express was better than Pizza Hut. I thought the
crusts were thinner and the toppings thicker. Also Pizza
Express is more upmarket and my friends seem to prefer it. My
tutor said I was begging the question: assuming to be
true what I was supposed to be proving. Did upmarket
necessarily mean better? She showed me a recent report in
Which? that contained a survey of pizza restaurants, showing
that on most counts Pizza Hut won more points. We can't talk
about conclusive proof in such matters, my tutor said, but a
survey using many people from a wide range, asking many
specific questions, is much more reliable evidence than I had
gathered. The opinions were more informed, clearly based on
facts.

I said, 'I would of course have argued more rigorously if I had
been writing an essay. It was only a discussion.'

She gave me a steely look. 'If you show little respect for

evidence in a class discussion,' she said, 'which expects you to treat it seriously, you will not be able to argue better in an essay.'

I wasn't going to argue with *her*.

In casual conversations we can get away with murder. But if you are strongly opinionated (or if you have strong opinions about certain subjects), it is wise to argue as rigorously in serious discussion as you do in essays. It is easy to get into bad habits — such as allowing the following **common flaws in argument** to appear: false syllogisms, begging the question, bias or sweeping generalisation, emotionally weighted language, special pleading, and non-sequiturs and red herrings. Here are examples:

False syllogisms
A syllogism is a deduction containing three parts, a major premise, a minor premise and a conclusion. A classical example is: 'All men are mortal. Greeks are men. Therefore Greeks are mortal.' A false syllogism or fallacy occurs when the major premise is false, even though the reasoning process is valid:

All students are lazy. John Anderson is a student. Therefore John Anderson is lazy.

The fallacy may occur when the minor premise doesn't follow the rules of logic:

Mentally ill people behave irrationally. John Anderson behaves irrationally. Therefore John Anderson is mentally ill.

'Behaving irrationally' in the minor premise doesn't have the same meaning as it does in the major premise.

Begging the question
Assuming to be true what you're supposed to be proving: 'I am quite sure that there are more drawbacks to watching TV than benefits.'

Bias, or sweeping generalisation
Ignoring the facts, especially those that support the opposing argument: 'Obviously women are less equal today than they were 20 years ago.'
Without evidence to back them up, avoid using persuader words such as 'obviously', 'clearly', 'plainly', 'surely'.

Emotionally weighted language
Commonly used by the prejudiced: 'The trouble with France is that the French are a charmless people who find it hard to appreciate the values of other countries: if it's not French, it's suspect.'

Special pleading
You have a vested interest in others accepting your argument: 'Quite clearly, the import duty on beers should be increased.' Your family owns a brewery.

Non-sequiturs and red herrings

Non sequitur is Latin for 'it doesn't follow'.

Since he started playing billiards his performance at work has deteriorated. The only solution is to stop the billiards.

A red herring is a similar kind of confusion: 'Of course she stole the boy's mobile. She has never stopped admiring it since she clapped eyes on it.'

Have another look at the essay outline of Appendix B and note where narration, description, exposition and argument techniques are required.

The place for emotion

Remember, though, that as the French philosopher Pascal said, the heart has its reasons which reason knows nothing of. Essays on such subjects as social problems justifiably use emotion to engage readers' sympathy and attention. The aim in arguing is to persuade, and sincerely evoking emotion will make the reader receptive to your reasoning. Discussing the homeless, the depressed, the wounded and all kinds of other unfortunates is unthinkable without bringing your heart into it. As long as, at the end of the argument, your head has ruled.

Practice

1. Rewrite this paragraph from the middle of a student's essay on 'The State of Britain's Prisons', making it

clearer: Assume the dates are correct. Reduce to about 60 words.

'How did conditions in Britain's prisons manage to get so bad? The prison population increased by almost half, from 44,000 in 1993 to 65,000 in 1999. It could be due to politicians like ex-Home Secretary Michael Howard who went on and on about the fact that sentencing should be tougher to discourage offenders from reoffending when they got out of prison. The prisons became overcrowded and conditions got worse and worse. In fact the number of female prisoners more than doubled in the period mentioned, while the percentage of defendants sentenced to prison in the Crown courts increased from 44 per cent to 61 per cent in 1999. Britain now has the second highest prison population in Western Europe. Although alternatives to prison such as rehabilitation and community service have been introduced, from the results of surveys and statistics and the evidence shown by the repetitive acts of repeat offenders, we have to say that prison is doing more harm than good'. (163 words)

2. Comment on the following common flaws in argument, showing where the flaw lies:

✓ **False syllogism.** She told her sister some time ago that if her husband gave up his job she would leave him. She did leave him. So her husband must have given up his job.

✓ **Begging the question.** It is quite obvious that the use of cctv in the streets will reduce the number of robberies.

✓ **Bias, or sweeping generalisation.** Clearly most of the promises the Liberal democrats are making are aimed at doing well at the next General Election.

✓ **Emotionally weighted language.** Young people today, I am told, are more honest, less hypocritical than they used to be. I call them irresponsible and bad mannered, and incapable of carrying on a joined-up conversation because their brains have been rotted by over-exposure to television. They are rarely given the guidance and good example they need from their parents so the parents must share the blame.

Chapter 6

Writing and Rewriting

When the reader's task is agreeable you can assume the writer has taken pains.

Here we devote our attention to:

♦ building strong paragraphs

♦ achieving sentence power

♦ discovering the right words

♦ matching style to content

♦ learning from criticism

When you have studied the topic, thought about it and put your ideas in order, **then is the time to start writing**. Your **writing style** will develop naturally out of what you want to say: it is not something you add on. The style will vary according to the complexity of the subject matter, but it will remain *your* style.

Books cannot teach you how to write. An Army training manual expresses concisely how to learn a skill:

> Tell me and I shall forget, show me and I shall remember, let me do it and I shall understand.

You must learn by writing, editing and rewriting, and by trying to write better next time. This book's aim is to guide you to the best strategy for you.

Case study

I am quite good at researching and making notes, I have plenty of ideas and I can plan an essay well. But when it comes to writing it up I easily get stuck.

First of all, I find it difficult to make a paragraph hang together – it tends to say one thing after another without showing how they add up. I can't seem to find the right linking words and phrases.

Secondly, my paragraphs and sentences tend to be too long because I can't find the precise words I want. I use too many clichés and sometimes mix metaphors. My tutor laughed loudly when I wrote: 'I always jump over a bridge that a lot of water has passed under' – but it didn't help my grade.

Building strong paragraphs

Overlong and disjointed paragraphs and sentences, and a reliance on clichés, betray a lack of word power. **It is word power that is the key to writing well.** Words breed thoughts, and thoughts breed words: it's an interactive process. The greater your vocabulary the more likely you are to do more thinking and to think better and more clearly; the more likely you are to **make the right connections,** essential for strong paragraphs. Those connections were illustrated in the 'keeping to the point' section of Chapter 5.

Achieving sentence power

Let's focus more closely on that basic principle, **as simple and as direct as possible.** Here are seven principles that will keep you on the right track:

1. **Average 15 to 20 words a sentence.** Some can be much shorter, a few can be much longer. Try to keep most sentences to one main point only, and to one subsidiary point.

2. **Vary the lengths, structures and emphases of your sentences.** 'This is the house that Jack built' is an excellent sentence. But a succession of sentences which have one main clause followed by one subordinate clause is monotonous. Especially when, like the previous one, they include the 'lazy which' (or 'lazy that').

    Replace such clauses with:

    a prepositional phrase: 'with one main clause . . . ' or:

    a participial phrase: 'having one main clause . . . ', 'containing . . . '

Change sentence structures in various ways. Just as in paragraphs, the most important words in a sentence are often first or last. Note how you can change the emphasis by changing the order. Consider these examples of rewriting, starting with the most common order of subject, verb, predicate:

(a) Excessive alcohol and lack of exercise can in a short period damage your memory and ability to focus on a subject.

(b) Damage to your memory and ability to focus on a subject: such penalties can quickly follow excessive alcohol and lack of exercise.

(c) The penalties for excessive alcohol . . . are a speedy damage to your memory . . . subject.

(d) It is damage to your memory and ability . . . that can quickly result from . . .

(e) Not only . . . but also . . .

(f) In a short period . . .

Practise doing this with your own sentences.

3. **Use active verbs rather than nouns or passive verbs.**
'This post **involves a combination of** administration and work in the field' is better expressed as 'This post **combines . . .**'

The first sentence is gobbledygook, which means using

overcomplicated language, and is a common fault in bureaucratic organisations. Gobbledygook also makes excessive use of passive verbs and (worse) impersonal passives.

Example: 'A decision has been made to . . .' (passive). Rewrite as: 'We have decided . . .'

Example: 'It is proposed that the replacement of the language courses will be carried out with some degree of urgency' (impersonal passive). Rewrite as: 'We intend to replace the language courses soon.'

4. **Give the result rather than the process. Example:** 'He tried and tried and tried again, using different methods at different times until he finally succeeded.' Rewrite as: 'He finally succeeded.'

5. **Be positive rather than negative. Example:** 'Don't use gobbledygook.' Rewrite as: 'Use plain English.'

6. **Keep related words together. Example:** 'There were a leisure centre and a cinema attracting many people from afar quite near the city centre.' Rewrite as: 'There were a leisure centre and a cinema quite near the city centre attracting many people from afar.'

Discovering the right words

The right word is the **precise** word. That adjective contains

the other essentials: conciseness, clarity, appropriateness.
Increase your word power by building up your active
vocabulary: read, use a good dictionary and thesaurus, and
put that increased vocabulary to use. You will find the right
words will come more often.

Whenever possible, use:

◆ short and familiar words rather than long and unfamiliar

◆ concrete words rather than abstract

◆ fresh words rather than stale.

Notice how the best writers, with all their differences, obey
these principles. The best speeches provide good models too,
of how to be instantly comprehensible, as do the pictures
simply and vividly painted of Christ's parables in the Bible:

> Consider the ravens, for they sow not, neither do they reap,
> neither have they storehouse nor barn, and God feedeth them.
> How much are you more valuable than they?

An economics essay off its guard might say the same thing
to much less effect:

> The excessive preoccupation with the accumulation of wealth
> betrays a reluctance in mankind to deposit the same amount of
> trust in Providence as is deposited by birds. Human beings
> should be appreciative of the fact that birds are provided with
> the necessities of life despite the fact that they show no such
> preoccupation.

Matching style to content

The academic essay at tertiary level has a tone of voice and choice of language more serious, more impersonal than the essays required in earlier years. That **impersonal passive** frowned at above will be needed from time to time. Guidance about such matters is given by good dictionaries, which indicate what they call **register:** telling you that particular words are formal, or informal, or slang, or old-fashioned, or obsolete. They may also give guidance on usage, pointing out that certain terms are offensive, and distinguishing between words often confused, such as **appraise** and **apprise.**

Learning from criticism

What you learn from the tutor's corrections and critical notes on your essay usually has to benefit your next essay. If you follow the guidance each time you should not fail to improve. That guidance is quite different from the general advice given to all before you embarked on the project. It is personal, specific, directly aimed at your weaknesses, and you can appreciate it fully because of the intellectual journey you have made.

> Listen to your tutor's criticism. It is intended to train you to become your own editor.

Editing may go on as you write, especially if you use a word processor. For convenience let's assume the main editing is done between first and second drafts (preferably after some feedback from fellow-student, or tutor if that's the system). **Leave the first draft for a few days if possible so that you see it with fresh eyes.**

Then edit cautiously, using a pencil and eraser in case you have second and third thoughts. Read through the essay three times to check content and flow, structure and style.

Checklist

Here is a guide to the editing process:

✓ **Content and flow**
Check the length and add or subtract to the content as necessary.

Check that all parts of the essay – paragraphs, sentences, words – are *relevant* to the topic.

Check that all main points made are backed up by *evidence* (eg facts, examples).

Check that sources are acknowledged.

Insert links if necessary to improve the flow.

✓ **Structure**
Check that the title, introduction and conclusion make a good team.

Check the overall structure with the plan and decide which to adjust before writing a new draft.

Check that the points made by each paragraph follow a logical pattern. Then check with the plan and decide which to adjust.

✓ **Style**
Underline words that need changing.

Underline sentences that need improving. There may be a need for more vigour and more variety, and there may be emphases in the wrong places.

Check that tone of voice and register are consistent. Check spelling, grammar, usage.

Practice

Rewrite these sentences as simply and concisely as possible:

(a) There is no doubt that today the trend is for women to delay having children

(b) I would describe the behaviour exhibited to be of a controversial nature.

(c) The book was from an educational viewpoint of an inadequate standard.

(d) There is a good deal of satisfaction with regard to the amount of work put in.

(e) The light bulbs you bought are of a different character from the ones we are in the habit of buying.

(f) Building the conservatory is not a practical proposition at the present moment in time.

(g) Matters appertaining to the student's application for a part-time job are being afforded full consideration by the committee.

(h) The questionnaire was designed as a means of consultation with employees with respect to any reservations concerning the proposal for a complete reorganisation of the department.

(i) The fact that Okonkwo is regarded as a successful man during most parts of the novel, is shown from the line 'one of the greatest men of his time', if Okonkwo was not respected so highly then his downfall and death would not be seen as such a tragedy, it is because of his immeasurable status among the society which makes Okonkwo's fate and the novel seem so tragic.

Chapter 7

Passing the Essay Exam

Writing essays well in exams is a special technique.
Prepare by writing essays under exam conditions.

Make sure while preparing that you are:

◆ **earning confidence**

◆ **adopting winning tactics**

◆ **spending time on review**

Clearly the expectations of an exam essay are not those of a term essay, even when research sources and notes may be brought in.

Exam essays must be written **at speed** and the polish possible in term essays with precise details of all sources isn't looked for. Nevertheless, you must deal with the topic **as comprehensively as time permits,** showing that you have absorbed the knowledge covered by the course and that you have applied that knowledge with some originality. **Presentation** must be clear, and handwriting legible.

These considerations need not be daunting **if you have**

prepared well. Make sure you know what ground the exam is to cover, by consulting a course outline in a handbook or as supplied by a tutor.

Check that the format of the exam will not differ from that of past papers. Resolve any doubts by talking to your tutor.

Case study

My poor showing in exam essays doesn't reflect my ability. I do much better in term essays. I have that sort of temperament. I like to get absorbed in a subject slowly and take twice as long as my fellow-students preparing for a term essay. I read around the topic, becoming fascinated by peripheral issues and taking too many notes, but in the end I'm rewarded by high grades. Unfortunately I don't seem to be able to change gear for the exam essay. I become nervous, and keep looking at my watch. I tend to panic and get confused. All my essay exams are submitted with one or more topics unfinished.

Earning confidence

Many students don't do justice to themselves at exams because they haven't developed the **special technique** required. That is like expecting to know how to ride a bike because you know how to walk. Here is a revision method that will prepare you to be confident at exams:

◆ **Learn at least as much of the subject as the exam will cover,** and some more.

◆ **Check it by testing,** orally or in writing, referring afterwards to notes and texts.

◆ **Apply your knowledge** in a mock exam.

1. **Learn it.** First read through your notes to make sure they are complete. Sources (texts and page numbers) should be indicated clearly. Check against texts any notes that you don't follow, or that appear to be inaccurately taken down.

   Study past exam papers. Would your notes have covered the ground? Do further reading to fill any gaps. Highlight main points if your notes are not on cards.

2. **Check it.** Make sure you know what ground is to be covered in the exam, and check that the format will follow that of past papers. Ask a fellow-student to question you on your notes and texts, or put them away and write out main points. Then check.

   Read through materials again to fill in any gaps in your knowledge. Check again.

3. **Apply it.** Make plans for topics of past papers. Then for practice complete one or two past papers under exam conditions: use notes for this only if they will be allowed at the exam. Then check against notes and texts to see how well you have done.

   If mock exams are arranged for you they may be sufficient practice. Check with your tutor.

Adopting winning tactics

Here is some general advice, which you must adapt to your own subject, needs and temperament:

◆ **Choosing and timing.** First read through all topics and instructions. Allocate a separate sheet for plans and rough work. Submit this with your paper at the end or, if you have time, transfer neatly any plans that might boost your grade if you haven't completed the writing up.

Decide how much time you will allow for each topic, and/or for planning and for revising at the end.

◆ **Quickly planning** the essay or essays. The advantage of planning more than one essay at the beginning is that if you run out of time at the end you can quickly flesh out a plan for the last topic. In the last resort you can submit the plan: you'll get some marks for it and it may give a good idea of your grasp of the topic.

A mind map may work well at an exam, or make a simple list of points or questions and indicate the order in which you will deal with them. Indicate in a plan at least one or two links and the conclusion: they make it easier to keep on track when you have to write quickly.

◆ **Thinking and writing quickly.** If you have prepared well and have learned to perform well at practice exams you will have a bedrock of confidence at the real exam. You will have earned it. Of course you will feel nervous — everybody does. In fact, a little nervousness is good for you on such occasions: it gets the adrenalin flowing, sharpens the mind, and enables you to think and write more quickly than usual.

Remember that the examiner will be looking for substance rather than elegance. Keep calm. If you find yourself tense, relax your muscles and take a few deep breaths. Do this several times during the exam.

If you go over the time you've allowed yourself for a topic and have still not completed it, **begin a new paragraph** so that you will be able to continue quickly when you return to it. Go on to the next topic. You will get more marks for two nearly completed topics than for one well done, completed topic plus one quite inadequate attempt. If towards the end you find yourself well behind, it may be best to complete a topic in notes or plan form.

Suppose, for example, you have attempted in an exam the essay outlined in Appendix B and cannot complete in time. Assume you have written out a briefer version of the outline given there. You have five minutes left and you realise it is not enough to produce a coherent account of what remains to be said. You do, however, have time to give the outline, from 'What must not be lost sight of is . . . .' to the end. That will produce a better grade than an essay which produces a rushed, incoherent ending.

Spending time on review

Ten minutes of editing at the end can make a significant difference to the grade. (Use the editing guide on pages 76–77.)

Checklist

✓ Discover by experiment what sort of study and planning methods described in this book will improve your exam performance.

✓ Don't cram your head with knowledge up to the last minute.

✓ Devise a timetable so that you fit in plenty of preparation study, testing and practice — before the exam.

Responses

Chapter 1

Your interpretations should follow these lines.

1. (a) 'My favourite restaurant'. Describe your favourite restaurant so that the place comes alive, showing why you prefer it to others.

   (b) 'If I were Prime Minister'. Explain what improvements you would make to the running of the country, concentrating on two or three areas. Choose from health, education, crime, drugs, transport.

   (c) 'Friendship'. What do you think is the essential quality of friendship? Illustrate by reference to your own experience.

2. What are the arguments against caring for the mentally ill in the community?

3. (a) Do you approve of competition in schools?

   (b) Celebrities have a *right* to a private life. Discuss.

(c) How important is the Fool's role in *King Lear*?

4. (a) Do you think it is a good idea to emphasise how school children compare with each other in the various subjects and in sports, etc., by listing them in order of merit (their positions in class)?

   (b) To what extent is it fair for the media to give details of the private lives of celebrities, which they would prefer not to be known? When is it 'in the public interest' for such matters to be publicised?

   (c) What function does the Fool play in the development of the plot of *King Lear*? How do his speeches help us to understand and be moved by the tragedy, to understand the protagonist and his misfortunes, and to make clear the relationships between the characters and the changing world they inhabit?

Chapter 2

1. Organic food has suddenly become big business, led by supermarkets and high street traders. (14 words)

2. UK farmers and growers, currently meeting 30 per cent of the demand, are converting land for organic produce. (18 words)

Chapter 3

2. Here is another pair of points for the TV topic:

Evidence of TV damage
TV documentaries on such subjects as anorexia,
mental illness, cruelty to children and new fashions
can have hidden agendas and can sacrifice the facts
to entertainment criteria. Important facts that don't
lend themselves to visual representation may be
neglected.

But:
A TV documentary on a current social problem can
create controversy and open people's minds to the
subject. That can be useful to the student of sociology
or social studies assessing public opinion. There may
also be insights into cases hard to come by in ordinary
experience or even in academic textbooks.

Chapter 5

1 The prison population in Britain increased from 44,000
in 1993 to 65,000 in 1999. Conditions have worsened
since. Why? Government emphasis on deterrence —
more and longer sentences — has produced unacceptable
overcrowding. The policy is not working, as is evidenced
by the number of repeat offenders. More attention is
needed on rehabilitation and on the community service
alternative. (58 words)

2. **False syllogism**

She may have left him for another reason and her husband may still be in his job.

Begging the question

Not necessarily. The number of robberies may increase in streets not covered by CCTV. A false sense of security might encourage more robberies.

Bias, or sweeping generalisations

A too cynical view. Some promises will be based on policies sincerely held, and most promises will be *partly* aimed at persuading everyone of the value of fulfilling them, whoever carries them out.

Emotionally weighted language

Applying strong terms of condemnation to all of the 'young people' today is poor argument. There is no sign of any evidence being weighed in the balance, when such extreme terms are used as *irresponsible*, *incapable*, *rotted* and *rarely*.

Chapter 6

(a)   Women today tend to delay having children.

(b)   The behaviour was controversial.

(c)   The book lacked educational value.

(d)   The work was satisfactory.

(e)   The light bulbs you bought are different from the ones we buy.

(f)   Building the conservatory is not practical now.

(g)   The committee is considering the student's application for a part-time job.

(h)   The questionnaire should reveal employees' views on the proposed reorganisation of the department.

(i)   It is a tragic novel because of the downfall and the suicide of the protagonist Okonkwu, who was revered as a great man by his society.

Formal Outline: Should charity be left to the state?

(*Linking phrases are in italics.*)

Introduction

1. Anecdote as hook.

2. Define 'charity' and 'charity organisation'. As examples: list main charities and indicate work of one or two. The picture has changed since start of Lottery.

3. The argument about current role of the State, and the effect of the receiving of Lottery funds. Argument for rationalising by much more centralising control.

4. Viewpoint: Answer to question is no. More government control desirable, but without losing benefits of individual efforts. *First the need to describe how the partnership works.*

I The way charity works

1. The government role in general: controls, central distribution. Within this, role of Lottery.

2. The Lottery and good causes: 25p out of every pound to 'good causes' via five organisations including the arts, sports, etc and Charities Board: give figures. Great benefits overall, but discourages direct giving of both government and individuals.

3. Gains by some charities, losses by others (interviews, figures). Also:

4. Pros and cons of the way charities work: inspired voluntary efforts; but danger of scams and embezzlements. *Combining state and local skills is the way forward.*

II Effective central/local control

1. Advantages of more centralised control: eg, prevention of scams. But two main disadvantages:

2. (a) How more centralised government control might produce more bureaucratic waste. Whereas:

   (b) Charities easier to organise locally, can identify local needs quickly.

3. Suggestions for getting the best of both worlds. *What is clear from above is that:*

III More regulation needed

1. Brief history of charities: attempts to regulate.

2. Current waste of funds on administration.

3. Scams can be hard to detect.

The role of the Lottery needs special attention:

IV The Lottery connection: suggested improvements

1. Contrast government, business and charities' views on how Lottery affects charities.

2. Their suggestions for improvements to the system.

3. Suggestions compared with press commentaries.

4. Sum up viewpoint on this aspect.

What must not be lost sight of is:

V The philosophical and psychological arguments

1. The State cannot legislate for morality.

2. 'Charity begins at home': implications for morality.

3. The dangers of encouraging materialism.

VI Conclusion

1. Sum up reforms needed.

2. Anecdote, quote or example showing a charity working at its best.